T0208062

Yes! I am a Military Child

A book for Military Brats

A Song and Story by
Laura Jo Ackerman

Archway Publishing books may be ordered through booksellers or by contacting:

Archway Publishing
1663 Liberty Drive
Bloomington, IN 47403
www.archwaypublishing.com
844-669-3957

Because of the dynamic nature of the Internet, any web addresses or links contained in this book may have changed since publication and may no longer be valid. The views expressed in this work are solely those of the author and do not necessarily reflect the views of the publisher, and the publisher hereby disclaims any responsibility for them.

Any people depicted in stock imagery provided by Getty Images are models, and such images are being used for illustrative purposes only.
Certain stock imagery © Getty Images.

Interior Image Credit: Dominique ZseDenny

ISBN: 978-1-6657-1724-3 (sc)
ISBN: 978-1-6657-1725-0 (e)

Print information available on the last page.

Archway Publishing rev. date: 11/21/2023

Yes! I am a Military Child

DEDICATION

My sincere thanks go out to our sons Jeffrey and Christopher. While our adventures were wild and sometimes unruly, we always managed to get through them. It has been an honor walking through life with you, and I am forever grateful to God for giving you to us. Having been born into a military family, you have served it well. We are amazed by both of you.

Yes, I am a military child,

Sometimes my life is really, really, wild.

My family sticks together like glue,

With hugs and kisses and giggles, too!

When Mom or Dad is far away,

I love them more and more each day.

I hold them in my heart so true,

Shhhhhhh!... I can hear them whisper 'I Love You'.

We move a lot, oh yes, we do,

I've had houses colored red,
green, white and blue.

Making friends is easy you see,

'Cause everyone moves around just like me!

My Mom and Dad are really strong,

This Military life can seem so long.

But in the end, this much is true:

My family sticks together,
My family sticks together,
My family sticks together,

Just like glue!

My Military Child Scrapbook

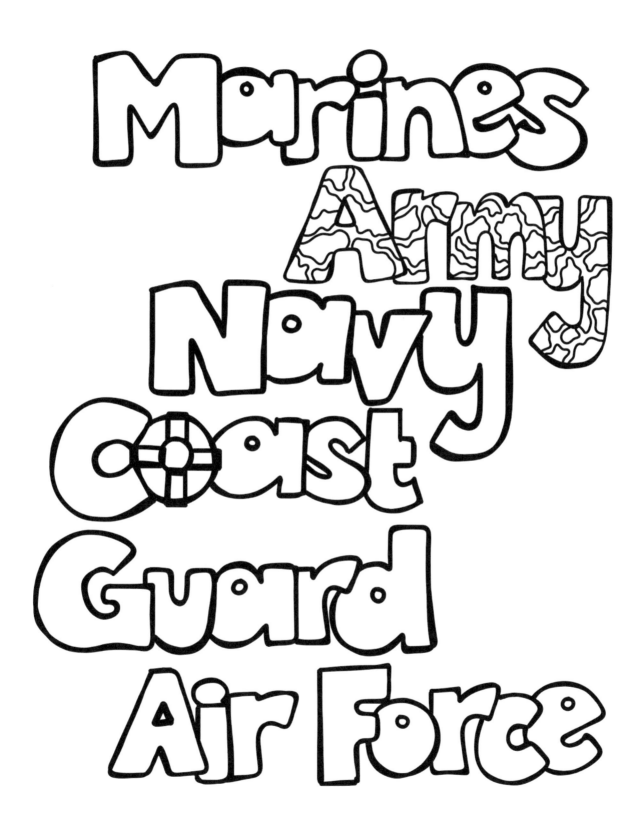

Marines
Army
Navy
Coast
Guard
Air Force

Draw a Picture of Yourself

Here is a place for you to draw a picture of you!

Draw a Picture of your Family

Add a family picture here, either by drawing it or by gluing it.

Draw a Picture of where you Live

What are some places where you have lived or stayed for a long time? Add a picture here by drawing or gluing it.

Tell a Story

Draw a picture of an adventure you have had with your family in a car or another form of transportation. You can write or tell a story about it.

_____

_____

_____

_____

_____

My Military Parent

Here you can draw a picture of your military family member. Draw more than one if you need to!

Free Page

This page has been saved for you. You are free to draw whatever you want.

MILITARY CHILD
THAT'S ME! Miss Laura &
the
Military Brats

About the Author:

Laura Jo Ackerman owns and operates Miss Laura's Music & Play in Cottage Grove, Minnesota. During her time at Fleet Activities Yokosuka, Japan, and Naval Station Great Lakes, Illinois, she volunteered in the MWR library as the Storytime Lady. In addition to her husband Tim, now a retired Navy oral surgeon, she has two wild and crazy boys. Teddy (Jeff) grew up dreaming of becoming a Marine, and he is still serving today, more than 10 years later. Having dreamed of a freestyle life after his childhood as a Brat, Christopher has become a lawyer's assistant, a private flight attendant, a homeowner at 21 and a highly skilled welder. In their own ways, they lived and travelled the military life together and are proud of the service they have given to their country.

About the Illustrator:

Dominique Gonzalez is proud to be a Military child. Her father served in the U.S. Air Force from before she was born until long after she grew up and moved out. Through her childhood she has moved all over the world with her family and has had the opportunity to experience the world from a unique perspective. She has been through moves that took her away from friends and familiar places, and deployments that took her father away from her, but through it all her family stayed strong, stayed together and stayed happy.

Printed in the United States
by Baker & Taylor Publisher Services